MEDITATION
ACTION
LIVELIHOOD
EFFORT
SPEECH
CALMEST
MU
CONCENTRATION
UNDERSTANDING
THOUGHT

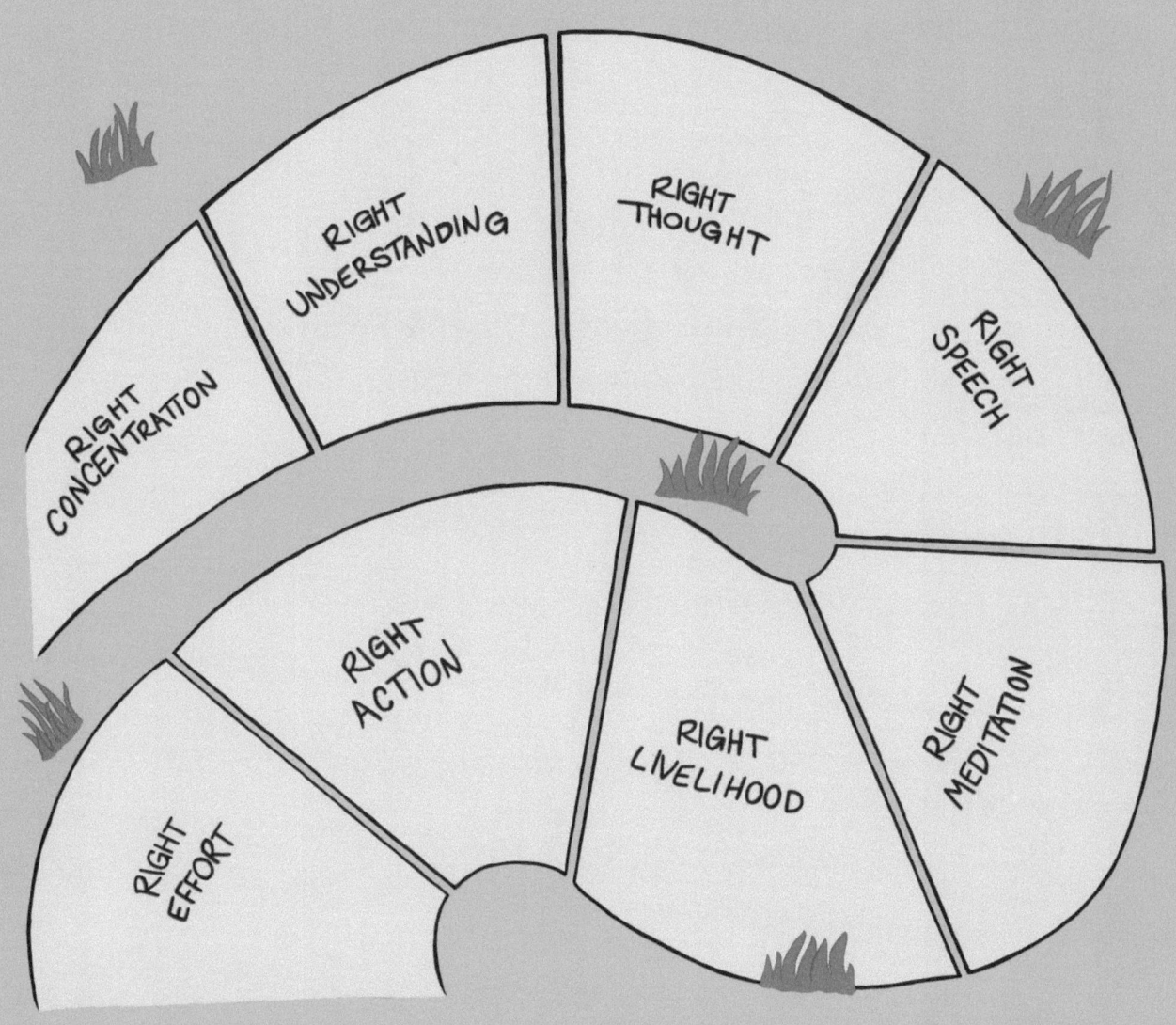

The Noble Eightfold Path is a beautiful idea as it imagines that we, as the individual, can change the world by first going within and changing oneself.

Remember, there are only two mistakes on this path.

Not starting one and not completing one.

One night Michael fell into a deep sleep, and when he opened his eyes, he realized he was no longer in his room, or in his bed. "Michael" he heard in a soft voice he never heard before. The voice sounded familiar.

All of a sudden Michael had a strange feeling. It was like being nowhere, yet everywhere all at the same time. He could see images of a world in the distant past. He saw his mother and father when they were children. He saw generations of grandparents he never met.

"Michael." the voice whispered again. Michael asked, "Who are you and where is that voice coming from?"

"I am your guardian ancestor, you have been asking many important questions and searching for answers. I have come to help guide you."

"Aww man, frowned Michael, I was beginning to believe I would never figure it out."

"Your existence on this planet is complicated, and it's success is based on a very delicate balance, one that is dependent on you to find, and keep."

"But I'm only a kid," said Michael.

"This I know, said the Guardian Ancestor, "you are also the one asking the questions. You will be able to answer those important questions as well as cure this world's ills, but first you must take this path and learn to go within. Be mindful that what appears simple is complicated and what seems complicated is simple"

Michael insisted "Can you please tell me, how I will know? Then the guardian ancestor faded away.

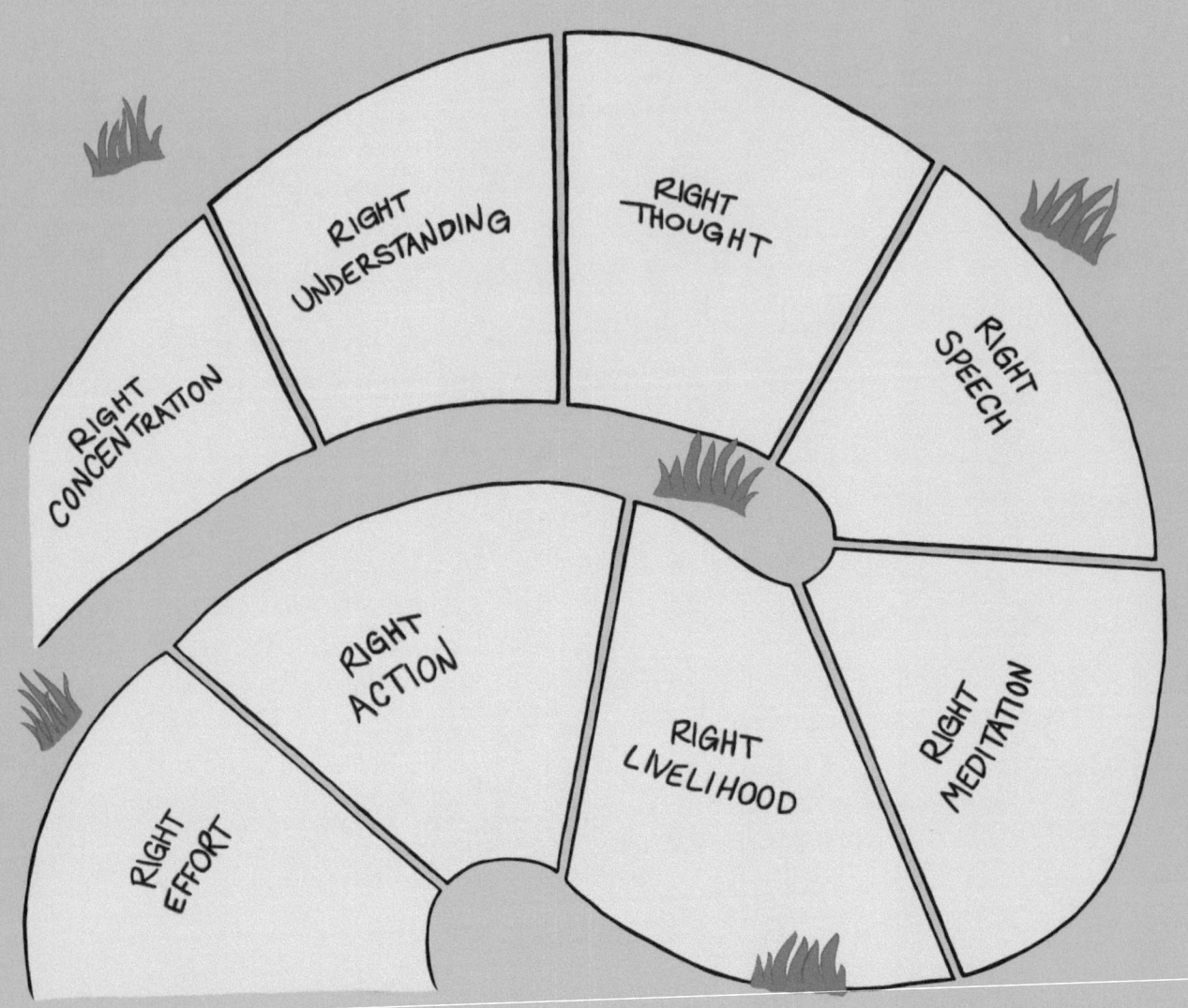

Michael sees a lot of things wrong with the world; things that do not make sense to him.

He wonders why some people struggle for money while others do not, or why some have nice homes and others do not!

He ponders why some people can go wherever they want but others cannot. Michael is seeing some of the world's problems but is having a hard time coming up with solutions.

Use the illustrative toolset to help Michael choose positive ways to deal with life's problems!

Michael is having a hard time concentrating with many distractions throughout the day.

Select one or more tools to help him concentrate along the way.

Take the time to think about each tool's use for Right Concentration.

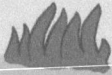

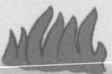

Michael feels lost and is unsure of the next actions he should take; should he act now or simply wait.

Select one or more tools to help Michael's actions secure a positive fate.

Take the time to think about each tool's use for Right Action.

Michael wants to be independent
with a livelihood that is honest.

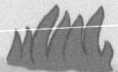

Select one or more tools to help
Michael live his purpose.

Take the time to think about each
tool's use for Right Livelihood.

Michael is learning meditation and how to be calm and still.

Select one or more tools to help Michael strengthen his meditation skills.

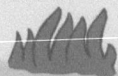

Take the time to think about each tool's use for Right Meditation.

Michael knows he must put forth an effort to meet his many goals!

Select one or more tools to help Michael maintain the right effort throughout the day.

Take the time to think about each tool's use for Right Effort.

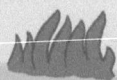

DAILY

EFFORT

DILIGENCE

PATIENCE

CONDITION & TRAIN

ACCOUNTABILITY

Michael knows that words are important so he practices speaking well!

Choose one or more tools to help Michael expand his reach through right speech!

Take the time to think about each tool's use for Right Speech.

Michael has a very big imagination and his thoughts run free. He loves to think of all he will grow up to be.

Select one or more tools to help Michael's lifelong ambitions by choosing right thoughts.

Take the time to think about each tool's use for Right Thought.

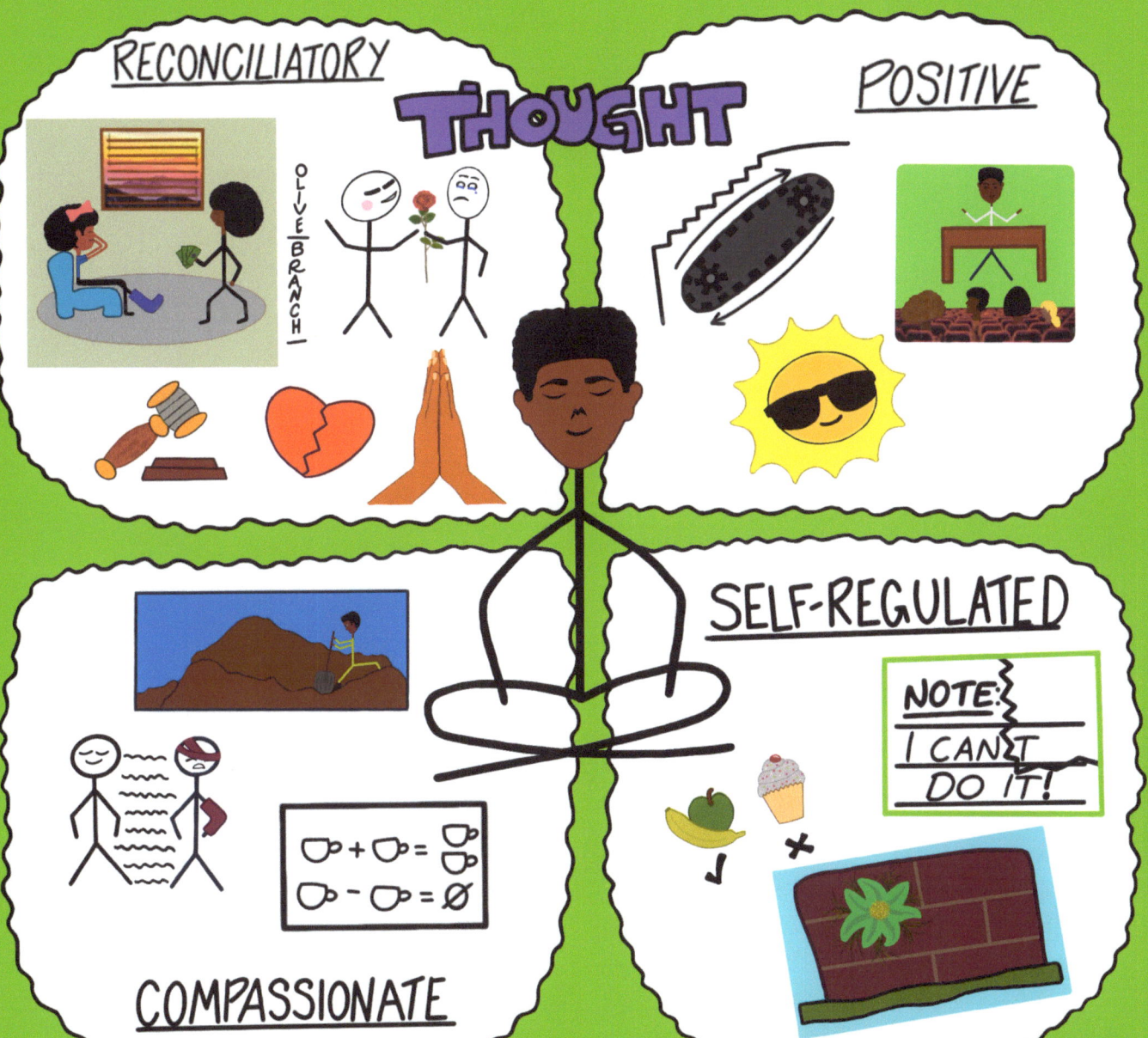

Michael understands that this path
never truly ends, and he can't wait to
walk it with all of his family and friends.

What are one or more tools we can all
use to create the right understanding?

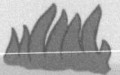

Take the time to think about each
tool's use for Right Understanding.

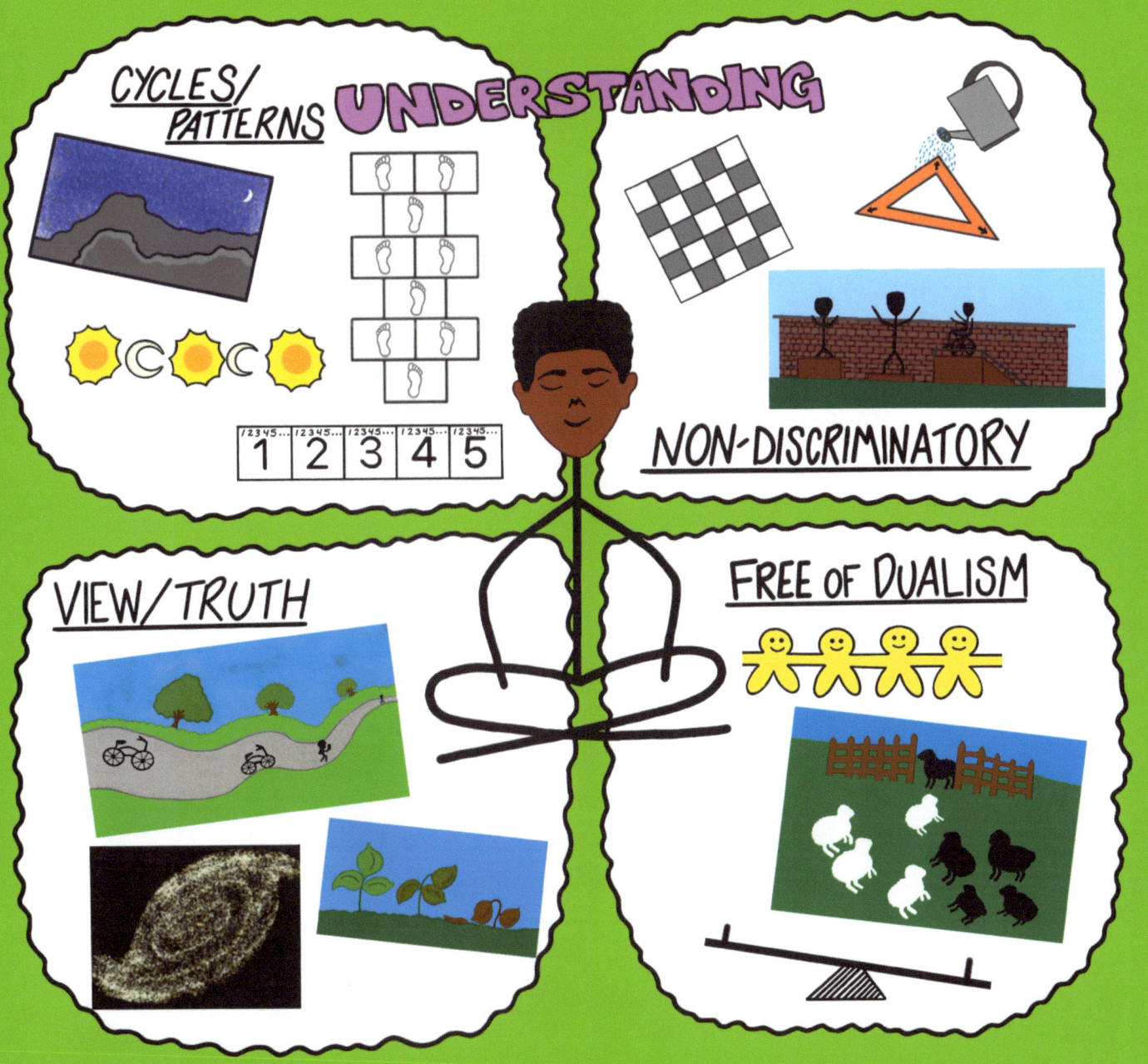

This interactive book pays homage to The Noble Eightfold Path and is meant to be used alone or hopefully shared with your loved ones. Be mindful that there is no particular order to move through the path, just have fun with it! Hopefully it will help you choose easy tools to be on your way to the Calmest U!

Remember:

Take the necessary time and strive to have **right concentration, action, livelihood, meditation, effort, speech, thought and understanding.**